BACK FROM NEAR EXTINCTION

# AMERICAN ALLIGATOR

by Carla Mooney

**Content Consultant**
James Perran Ross
Associate Scientist
Wildlife Ecology and Conservation
University of Florida

**Core Library**

An Imprint of Abdo Publishing
abdopublishing.com

abdopublishing.com

Published by Abdo Publishing, a division of ABDO, PO Box 398166, Minneapolis, Minnesota 55439. Copyright © 2017 by Abdo Consulting Group, Inc. International copyrights reserved in all countries. No part of this book may be reproduced in any form without written permission from the publisher. Core Library™ is a trademark and logo of Abdo Publishing.

Printed in the United States of America, North Mankato, Minnesota
092016
012017

Cover Photo: Arto Hakola/Shutterstock Images
Interior Photos: Arto Hakola/Shutterstock Images, 1; Mauro Rodrigues/Shutterstock Images, 4; Superstock/Glow Images, 7, 10; Leonardo Gonzalez/Shutterstock Images, 8, 45; iStockphoto/Thinkstock, 12, 43; Shutterstock Images, 14; Red Line Editorial, 17; Richard A McMillin/Shutterstock Images, 19; Underwood Archives/UIG/Bridgeman Images, 22; Gerald Herbert/AP Images, 26; Dmitry Mozhzherin/Shutterstock Images, 29; Heiko Kiera/Shutterstock Images, 32; J. Pat Carter/AP Images, 37; Orhan Cam/Shutterstock Images, 39; Andy Lidstone/Shutterstock Images, 40

Editor: Megan Anderson
Series Designer: Jake Nordby

**Publisher's Cataloging-in-Publication Data**

Names: Mooney, Carla, author.
Title: American alligator / by Carla Mooney.
Description: Minneapolis, MN : Abdo Publishing, 2017. | Series: Back from near
    extinction | Includes bibliographical references and index.
Identifiers: LCCN 2016945397 | ISBN 9781680784626 (lib. bdg.) |
    ISBN 9781680798470 (ebook)
Subjects:  LCSH: American alligator--Juvenile literature.
Classification: DDC 597.98--dc23
LC record available at http://lccn.loc.gov/2016945397

# CONTENTS

# CHAPTER ONE

# THE AMERICAN ALLIGATOR

The American alligator rests on the sunny bank of a Louisiana swamp. He cannot control his own body temperature, so the alligator uses the sun to warm up. After hours of sleep, the alligator rises to his feet. Slowly, he walks on his four short legs toward the water's edge. Then he slides into the swamp and disappears.

Alligators bask in the sun to warm themselves.

## Cold Weather

When the weather gets cold, American alligators slow down and become dormant. If the temperature dips below 70 degrees Fahrenheit (21°C), they stop feeding. At extremely warm or cold temperatures, alligators dig a den or burrow in the bank of a river, pond, or lake. It can be as long as 65 feet (20 m). The den provides alligators with a stable temperature and protection. The alligator's metabolism slows down. It does not breathe as often. While dormant, alligators live off their own fat. They do not need to feed. They rarely stay in a den for longer than a week or two.

Once in the water, the alligator is a powerful swimmer. He uses his tail to propel himself while his webbed feet steer. The alligator moves very quickly in the water. He can reach speeds of up to 20 miles per hour (32 km/h) or more. When the alligator surfaces, only his eyes and nostrils are above the water. Hidden in the swamp, he waits.

As he floats in the water, the alligator begins to hunt. He uses his senses of sight and smell to search for prey. When an unsuspecting fish

When it is hot, an alligator will sometimes have its mouth open. This is one way an alligator cools itself.

swims by, the alligator snaps it up in his powerful jaws. He swallows the prey whole.

The alligator can spend many hours in the water. When he wants to warm up again, he moves back to the shoreline. He rests in a sunny spot near the water's edge. At one point, an unlucky raccoon comes for a drink. The alligator moves in a short burst of speed toward the raccoon. He traps the prey and grabs it in

Alligators have both inner and outer eyelids. The inner eyelids help protect an alligator's eyes underwater.

his jaws. He slides into the water, pulling the prey with him. He drowns it in the water and swallows it.

The alligator returns to the bank. A few other alligators gather nearby to bask in the sun. Yet the hunter does not stay with the group. He will move around by himself. When he is ready to hunt again, he prefers to return to the water alone.

## Threats to the Alligator

The American alligator is an intimidating predator. It has an armored body, a muscular tail, and powerful jaws. These features have made it the top predator in its habitat for millions of years. In fact, scientists believe this alligator species is more than 150 million years old. It was alive at the time of the dinosaurs. When dinosaurs went extinct 65 million years ago, the American alligator survived.

## Social Interactions

Male and female alligators are often seen basking together. Alligators use specific vocalizations to coordinate activity with one another and signal danger. During mating season, large male alligators fight each other to establish dominance. Males attract females with roars, rumbles, and head slaps. Males and females develop bonds by swimming together, blowing bubbles, and nudging snouts. Newly hatched alligators remain together in groups called pods for several months with their mother nearby. Eventually the alligators in these groups disperse when they are one or two years old. Alligators will tolerate others living nearby.

Conservation efforts have helped the number of alligators grow to approximately 5 million today.

But in the past 150 years, the survival of the American alligator has been threatened. Unregulated hunting for alligator skins caused many alligators to die. In addition, humans built communities and moved onto land occupied by alligators. Humans and alligators came into contact more and more. Changes to their habitats also threatened the alligators. But conservation and education efforts have helped bring alligators back from the threat of extinction.

## FURTHER EVIDENCE

Chapter One describes some characteristics of the American alligator and the threats they face. What do you think is the main point of the chapter? What evidence was given to support that point? Visit the website below to learn more about American alligators. Does the information on the website support the main point in this chapter? Write a few sentences using new information from the website as evidence to support the main point in this chapter.

**General Alligator Information**
mycorelibrary.com/american-alligator

# CHAPTER TWO

# A SNAPSHOT OF THE ALLIGATOR

The American alligator is the largest reptile in North America. Adult males can reach a size between 10 and 15 feet (3–4.6 m) long. They can weigh as much as 1,000 pounds (453 kg). Female alligators are a little bit smaller. They can measure up to approximately 9.8 feet (3 m) in length. About half of the alligator's length is its powerful tail.

The American alligator's tough skin helps it withstand the sun.

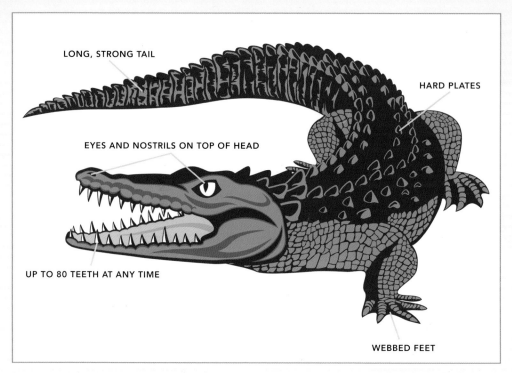

LONG, STRONG TAIL

HARD PLATES

EYES AND NOSTRILS ON TOP OF HEAD

UP TO 80 TEETH AT ANY TIME

WEBBED FEET

**American Alligator**
The alligator's body is well suited for its habitat. This diagram shows the different physical characteristics of an alligator. How does each characteristic help it survive in the wild?

Although they have long bodies, American alligators have very short legs. They generally move quite slowly on land. However, they are able to run quickly over a short distance, rising straight up on their legs. Their front feet have five toes, while the back feet have four. Webbed feet help the alligator swim and steer.

Armor-like skin protects an alligator's body. The skin is covered in hard bony plates called scutes. Adult alligators are olive brown or black with a creamy-white underside. Young alligators have bright yellow bands around their bodies and tails. Humans value alligator skin. They use it to make leather goods, such as purses, belts, and shoes.

Alligators have broad heads and snouts. They have nostrils at the front ends of their snouts. This allows alligators to breathe while the rest of their bodies are underwater. Only the tip of their snouts rest above the water's surface.

## Communication

American alligators are very vocal. This starts when they are still inside eggs. When they are ready to hatch, they make high-pitched noises. Adult alligators bellow and roar at one another. An alligator's bellow is loud and can be heard up to 165 yards (150 m) away. Alligators make sounds called *chumpfs* when courting. It sounds like a mix of a cough and a purr. Alligators can also communicate with low-frequency sounds that humans cannot hear.

An alligator's eyes are on the top of its head. When it is in the water, it can swim with just the top of its head peeking above the surface. This helps the alligator sneak up on its prey. The alligator has an extra eyelid on each eye. The eyelid is clear so the alligator can see underwater. An alligator's large eyes give it clear night vision to see prey.

## Habitat

Alligators live in the southeastern United States. They can be found from North Carolina to Texas. Most alligators live in Florida and Louisiana. Because alligators cannot generate heat internally, they depend on external heat. For that reason, alligators live in warm-weather climates. The warm weather helps them keep their body temperature up. Alligators live on land and in water. They usually live in slow-moving freshwater rivers. They also live in freshwater lakes, ponds, marshes, swamps, and wetlands. Alligators do not live in bodies of salt water, such as the ocean. They do not have salt glands.

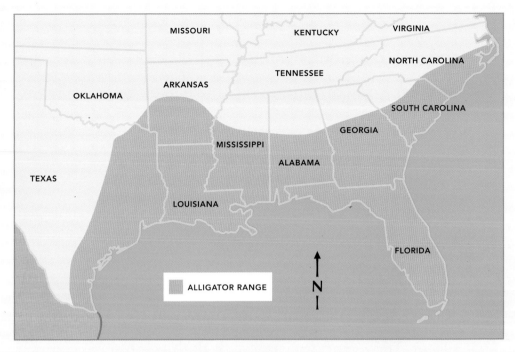

## Where Does the Alligator Live?

The American alligator can be found from northeastern North Carolina to eastern Texas. Sometimes alligators have been found up the Mississippi River in Arkansas and almost as far north as Virginia. They have also been found occasionally in the lower Rio Grande along the US border with Mexico. What makes these areas ideal places for alligators to live?

These body parts help animals get rid of extra salt from their bodies. As a result, alligators can tolerate salt water only for short periods of time.

American alligators dig dens using their snouts and tails. They use these dens for shelter and during very hot or very cold temperatures. If the water where they live dries out, alligators will walk or swim to another body of water. They have even been found swimming in backyard swimming pools.

## Hunting and Diet

Alligators are carnivores. They eat fish, snails, birds, frogs, and small mammals that come to the water's edge. They have powerful jaws that can crack a turtle's shell. Alligators hunt mostly at night in the water. They snap up prey with their mighty jaws and sharp teeth. An alligator has up to 80 teeth in its mouth. When a tooth wears down, a new one grows in its place. Over its life span, an alligator may go through 2,000 to 3,000 teeth.

If the prey is small, an alligator will swallow it whole. If the prey is too large to swallow, the alligator will tear it into smaller pieces. Sometimes, alligators will hold prey in their jaws until it breaks down enough to swallow. Alligators wait for unsuspecting prey to come to the water to drink. They grab the prey and drag it underwater until it drowns.

An American alligator eats a spiny soft-shell turtle at Brazos Bend Park in Texas.

## Male or Female?

Whether an alligator egg becomes a male or female alligator depends on the temperature. Eggs that develop in hotter temperatures (90 to 93 degrees Fahrenheit [32–34°C]) become male alligators. Eggs that develop in cooler temperatures (82 to 86 degrees Fahrenheit [28–30°C]) become female alligators. For temperatures in between, eggs can become either male or female alligators. Once they hatch, little alligators grow very quickly. They can grow an average of one foot (0.3 m) per year until they reach their adult size.

## Behavior

During very cold and very hot weather, an alligator may dig a gator hole in the mud. The gator hole often fills with water. It creates a habitat for fish and other animals. The alligator does not hibernate. But it may become dormant during very cold weather.

During breeding season, a female alligator chooses a protected spot in or near the water. She builds a nest with sticks, leaves, and mud. She lays 35 to 50 eggs in the nest, usually in late June or early July. The eggs incubate for approximately 65 days. Around the end of August, the hatchlings make noises inside the eggs. This attracts the mother's attention. When most of the eggs have cracked, the mother carries each egg to the water. She carefully helps eggs that haven't cracked by rolling them in her mouth. The mother also discards any eggs that won't live. Baby alligators are approximately six to eight inches (15–20 cm) long. Mother alligators defend their babies for the first few months. Even so, predators, such as birds and raccoons, will eat many of the baby alligators.

## EXPLORE ONLINE

The website below has information about the biology and ecology of the American alligator. As you know, every source is different. How is the information at the website different from the information in this chapter? What information is the same? What information did you learn from the website?

### American Alligator: Species Profile
mycorelibrary.com/american-alligator

# CHAPTER THREE

# THREATS TO SURVIVAL

The alligator species is more than 150 million years old. Native Americans who lived in the southeastern United States hunted and killed alligators. They ate their meat. They used alligator skins to make drums. Some made necklaces from alligator teeth and bones.

In the 1600s, European explorers arrived in America. They thought alligators were scary monsters.

A Seminole Native American shows his children how to dry an alligator hide in the 1930s.

They feared them. Because they were afraid of alligator attacks, many settlers killed alligators.

## Hunted for Their Skins

In the 1800s, more people started killing alligators for their skins. At the time, leather clothing and accessories were very fashionable. This trend started in Louisiana, then spread to designers in Europe. They used alligator leather to make clothing, purses, shoes, boots, and belts. As a result, alligator leather was in high demand. Selling alligator skins became a very profitable trade. American hunters killed many alligators and sold their skins to Europeans.

During the American Civil War (1861–1865), the Confederate army had a leather shortage. Thousands of alligators were killed to make leather shoes, boots, and saddles for Confederate soldiers. In the late 1800s, US factories started using alligator skins to make clothing and purses.

Hunting of alligators increased. At the time, hunting was unregulated. There were no laws on how many alligators could be killed. Soon, hunters were killing large numbers of alligators each year to sell their skins. By the mid-1900s, hunters had killed millions of alligators. The number of alligators dramatically declined. In some areas, it was feared that these ancient animals would go extinct.

## Habitat Loss and Other Threats

Hunting was not the only threat to American alligators. They were also losing their homes. More people were moving to the southeastern United States. They built homes and businesses on land that was part of the alligator's natural habitat.

## Keystone Species

Alligators are an important part of their ecosystem. They are called a keystone species. This means they have a strong influence on other species in their ecosystem. If the alligator species is removed from the ecosystem, it can have a ripple effect on the other animals and plants. If a keystone species disappears, it could affect other species that rely on it to survive. These other species in the ecosystem could also disappear and become extinct.

An alligator interrupts a PGA golf tournament in Avondale, Louisiana.

This also resulted in pollution in the wetlands where the alligators lived. The alligators were forced to find new places to live. Moving to new habitats made alligators more vulnerable to predators. Alligator eggs were at risk from attacks by raccoons, bears, and otters in their new habitats. Young alligators faced more danger from birds and bigger alligators.

As alligators were forced to find new homes, more humans were moving into nearby areas. More alligators came in contact with humans. People found alligators in their swimming pools, backyards, and golf courses. When left alone, alligators will usually stay away from humans. But because many people were afraid of alligators, they killed the animals.

Other times, humans killed alligators because they mistook them for crocodiles. It can be difficult for the average person to tell the difference between a crocodile and alligator. Crocodiles are typically more aggressive than alligators. Sometimes hunters intending to kill a crocodile killed an alligator instead.

## Alligator vs. Crocodile

Alligators and crocodiles are both reptiles. They have many similarities, but also several important differences. Alligator heads are shorter and wider than those of crocodiles. Their heads are U-shaped, compared to a crocodile's more V-shaped head. Alligators have two distinct nostrils, while crocodile nostrils are close together. The alligators typically have darker skin compared to crocodiles. Alligators also prefer to live in freshwater, while some species of crocodile live in salt water. Both look threatening, but alligators are actually less aggressive than crocodiles. And while alligators are only found in the United States and China, crocodiles live in many other places around the world.

Foreign species have also been introduced into alligator habitats. This poses new threats to alligators, their nests, and their eggs. Argentine fire ants invade alligator nests and kill eggs and hatchlings. Exotic reptiles, such as African monitor lizards and South American tegu lizards, were introduced to the alligator habitat. They are also predators of alligator eggs and hatchlings. Large Burmese pythons in the Florida Everglades

A crocodile, shown here, has more teeth visible when its mouth is closed compared to an alligator.

are new predators affecting birds, mammals, and alligators.

## Endangered Species

By the early 1960s, the American alligator was in trouble. Too many were killed by hunting and habitat loss. Populations of alligators in the wild were at all-time lows. In some regions, the alligator had already disappeared entirely. In 1967 the federal government listed the American alligator as endangered. This meant that it was in danger of becoming extinct. At first, commercial and recreational hunting were outlawed. But something more needed to be done to protect these ancient reptiles.

A US Geological Survey (USGS) study of water conditions in the Everglades showed how habitat changes could impact alligators:

> [As] water conditions change in the . . . Everglades ecosystem, gators are one of the key species that could be affected.
>
> [The] number of American alligators observed . . . dropped following dry years, and then appeared to recover in later non-dry years. The decrease in alligators appeared proportional to the intensity of the dry event. . . .
>
> "Alligator behavior and habitat use is linked to hydrology, and when that hydrology changes, alligator behavior and habitat can change," said USGS research ecologist Hardin Waddle, lead author of the study. "They don't need it wet all the time, but if dry events increase in frequency and intensity, this could be problematic for alligator numbers in the greater Everglades ecosystem."

Source: "Everglades' Alligator Numbers Drop after Dry Years." US Geological Survey. US Geological Survey, October 28, 2015. Web. Accessed June 21, 2016.

## Consider Your Audience

Review this passage. Think about how to explain it to a different audience, such as your classmates or a younger sibling. Write a blog post explaining the same information for the new audience. What is the best way to get your point across to this audience?

# CHAPTER FOUR

# CONSERVATION EFFORTS

In the 1960s, the federal and state governments began to take action to save the American alligator. Florida banned alligator hunting in 1961. Louisiana passed a hunting ban in 1962. Even with these laws, poachers continued to hunt alligators illegally. They killed them and sold their skins to traders. Alligator populations continued to decline.

A baby alligator basks in the Florida Everglades. The alligator became Florida's official state reptile in 1987.

## The Endangered Species Act

Passed by Congress in 1973, the Endangered Species Act helps the federal government protect endangered and threatened species. An endangered species is at risk of becoming extinct in all or most of its range. A threatened species is likely to become endangered in the near future. The act makes it against the law for anyone to harm or take a member of the listed species. This includes potentially harming a species by damaging a critical habitat. The ESA also helps the government assist state agencies in managing wildlife species. As of May 2016, approximately 1,600 animal and plant species were listed as threatened or endangered.

## Protecting the Alligator

In the 1960s and 1970s, the federal government passed several laws to protect endangered animals, including the American alligator. Congress passed the Endangered Species Preservation Act in 1966. This act would eventually become the Endangered Species Act of 1973. This federal act listed American alligators as endangered in 1967. The species was thought to be in danger of becoming extinct.

In 1969 the federal government made it illegal to buy and sell alligators. Under the new laws, law enforcement increased efforts to stop poachers and traders. Some traders were fined. Others were put in jail. Faced with these punishments, traders stopped buying alligator skins from hunters. Louisiana and Florida pressured the federal government to lift the ban. Instead, people were given economic reasons to preserve the alligator habitat. These included alligator farms, egg collection, and hunting. Between 1974 and 1978, alligator populations in parts of Louisiana, Texas, and Florida were reclassified as threatened.

The US Fish and Wildlife Service also worked with state wildlife agencies to restore alligators. Alligators from healthy populations were moved to areas where there were few alligators or where they had disappeared. State agencies monitored the relocated alligators to make sure they were doing well.

These efforts allowed the alligator population to grow again. As the alligators came back, states

## Alligator Farms

The American alligator has made a comeback. The population has grown into the millions. Because alligators have recovered so well, some states allow people to set up alligator farms. An alligator farm raises alligator eggs collected in the wild for meat, leather, and other goods. Alligator farming is a big business. Alligator skin can be sold to make purses, coats, shoes, and other items. Some parts of the alligator are sold for meat. Claws can be turned into backscratchers. Bones can be ground and used as fertilizer. In Louisiana alone, alligator products earn approximately $60 to $70 million annually.

created programs to monitor and remove alligators harmful to humans. Officials watched alligator populations closely. They made sure that the alligators continued to grow in numbers. By 1987, the US Fish and Wildlife Service declared that the American alligator was fully recovered throughout its range. It was no longer in danger of becoming extinct. The federal government removed the alligator from the threatened and endangered species list.

Officials collect alligator eggs in the Everglades. The top of each egg is marked during collection.

## Ongoing Regulation

Today the federal and state governments still protect the American alligator. The Endangered Species Act classifies the alligator as "threatened due to similarity of appearance." Caimans are species related to alligators. They are found in South and Central

America. Caimans and similar species of crocodiles are still in danger of becoming extinct. Alligators are easily mistaken for these animals. That means they are considered threatened. This status allows states to manage alligator populations. The government still regulates the sale of alligator skins and products.

Currently millions of alligators live in the southeastern United States. In some states, alligators can be killed using controlled hunts. In other states, alligators are bred in captivity for their meat and skins. Products from alligator farms are sold legally. Some of the money raised is used for conservation efforts for alligators in the wild.

## Long-Term Survival

The future looks bright for the American alligator. There are approximately 5 million alligators in the southeastern United States. But the alligator still faces challenges. People still push alligators off their lands. Pollution also continues to damage the alligator's habitat as these populations continue to grow.

The American alligator population has made a remarkable recovery.

Experts hope education can help humans and alligators coexist as they continue to come into contact.

Alligators and humans are more likely to meet. States with alligator populations are working to educate the public on how to successfully live with alligators. They also work to control alligator populations through legal hunts and egg collection. Conservationists hope alligators and humans can live together in peace.

The Florida Fish and Wildlife Conservation Commission (FWC) receives an average of 16,000 alligator-related complaints each year. The FWC issued a fact sheet with several alligator safety tips:

> *Do not swim outside of posted swimming areas or in waters that might be inhabited by large alligators.*
>
> *Alligators are most active between dusk and dawn. Therefore, avoid swimming at night.*
>
> *Dogs and cats are similar in size to the natural prey of alligators. Don't allow pets to swim, exercise or drink in or near waters that may contain alligators. . . .*
>
> *Leave alligators alone. State law prohibits killing, harassing or possessing alligators. . . .*
>
> *Never feed alligators—it's dangerous and illegal. When fed, alligators can overcome their natural wariness and learn to associate people with food. . . .*

Source: *"A Guide to Living with Alligators."* Florida Fish and Wildlife Commission. *Florida Fish and Wildlife Commission, February 2012. Web. Accessed June 21, 2016.*

## What's the Big Idea?

Take a close look at the alligator safety tips from the FWC. What is the main idea? What evidence supports this point? Write a few sentences showing how the FWC uses evidence to support its main point.

# SPECIES OVERVIEW

- American alligator

- *Alligator mississippiensis*

- 10 to 15 feet (3–4.6 m) for males; 9.8 feet (3 m) for females
- 200 to 300 pounds (91–136 kg) for females; 500 to 600 pounds (226–272 kg) for males

- Olive brown or black with a creamy-white underside

- Fish, snails, reptiles, birds, frogs, and small mammals

- 35 to 50 years in the wild; 65 to 80 years in captivity

## Habitat

- Freshwater lakes, rivers, ponds, marshes, and wetlands

## Threats

- Habitat loss, pollution in habitat, and conflicts with people
- Endangered status: threatened by similarity of appearance

# STOP AND THINK

## Why Do I Care?

This book discusses how conservation efforts brought American alligators back from the brink of extinction. What types of conservation work have you seen in your community? How has conservation improved our lives? Think about two or three ways the work of conservationists connects to your own life. Give examples of parts of your life that have been enhanced by conservation.

## Take a Stand

This book discusses alligators and conservation. Several strategies have been used to protect the American alligator. Take a position on the conservation efforts used to protect alligators, and write a short essay detailing your opinion, reasons for your opinion, and facts and details that support those reasons.

## You Are There

Imagine you work as a conservationist in the Florida Everglades. Write 300 words describing your life. What do you see happening in the wetlands? How do you interact with alligators? What training activities do you perform to prepare you to work with alligators?

## Say What?

Reading about animal conservation efforts can mean learning new vocabulary. Find five words in this book that you have never seen or heard before. Use a dictionary to find out what they mean. Then write the meanings in your own words and use each word in a new sentence.

# GLOSSARY

**burrow**
a hole or tunnel made in the ground by an animal

**carnivore**
an animal that eats other animals for food

**conservation**
preserving and protecting something

**dominance**
having power or control over something else

**dormant**
the state of normal physical functions being slowed down

**endangered**
being at risk of becoming extinct

**habitat**
a place in nature where animals or plants usually live

**metabolism**
all the chemical reactions in the body that are involved with living

**poachers**
people who illegally hunt wild animals

**predator**
an animal that hunts and eats other animals

**prey**
an animal that is hunted by other animals for food

**traders**
people who exchange goods for other goods

**unregulated**
not controlled by the government

# LEARN MORE

## Books

Bell, Samantha S. *12 Reptiles Back from the Brink.* North Mankato, MN: 12 Story Library, 2015.

Furstinger, Nancy. *Alligators.* Minneapolis, MN: Abdo, 2014.

Marsh, Laura. *Alligators and Crocodiles.* Washington, DC: National Geographic, 2015.

## Websites

To learn more about Back from Near Extinction, visit **booklinks.abdopublishing.com**. These links are routinely monitored and updated to provide the most current information available.

Visit **mycorelibrary.com** for free additional tools for teachers and students.

# INDEX

# ABOUT THE AUTHOR

Carla Mooney is the author of several books for young readers. She loves investigating and learning about people, places, and animals. A graduate of the University of Pennsylvania, she lives in Pittsburgh, Pennsylvania, with her husband, three children, and dog.